For the Living

By Edgar N. Jackson

This Is My Faith (1951), *Abingdon*
How to Preach to People's Needs (1956), *Abingdon*
Understanding Grief (1957), *Abingdon*
A Psychology For Preaching (1960), *Channel*
You and Your Grief (1961), *Channel*
Facing Ourselves (1961), *Abingdon*
The Pastor and His People (1962), *Channel*

EDGAR N. JACKSON

For the Living

INTRODUCTION BY

JAMES A. KNIGHT, B.D., M.D.

*Published by Channel Press,
An Affiliate of Meredith Press*

FOR THE LIVING

Copyright © 1963 by Edgar N. Jackson

Library of Congress Catalog Card Number: 63-23361

Preface

During the last few years I have lectured before tens of thousands of clergymen, chaplains, seminarians, physicians, medical and psychiatric students, nurses and funeral directors on the subject of grief and of providing help to bereaved persons facing this major emotional crisis of their lives.

In the free and vigorous discussion that followed these lectures, many questions were asked. These were questions that needed to be asked—and I believe them to have been the sort of questions you yourself might now ask were we sitting together and speaking together. You deserve honest and objective answers.

I have tried to address myself to such matters in the pages that follow, with the hope that the inquiries and information that has absorbed professional groups will be of similar interest to the general reading public.

EDGAR N. JACKSON

Chelsea, Vermont

Contents

Introduction

The crisis of bereavement is a topic that should command the most serious psychological and theological consideration. Associated with this crisis are the rites and ceremonies surrounding death, the funeral, and the work of mourning.

The medical profession is beginning to pay increasing attention to both normal and pathological grief, and to its significance as one of the causative factors in the development of psychosomatic illnesses. In fact, the major direction in psychosomatic medicine today evolves around grief, loss and separation as contributing factors in the development of a multitude of physical and emotional disorders. Denial of grief and a refusal to do "the work of mourning" are often involved in the development of such psychophysiologic illnesses as ulcerative colitis and duodenal ulcer, or hostile and aggressive acts against society, as well as mental illnesses.

Dr. Jackson brings to the topics discussed in this book a knowledge and wisdom seldom equalled. His more than thirty years in the pastorate, his extensive training and experience in psychotherapy, and his scholarly and practical writings in the management of grief all qualify him for the profoundly significant leadership he is furnishing in this field.

Dr. Jackson's books, *Understanding Grief* and *You and Your Grief,* are widely recognized. Members of the medical profession, and particularly those in psychiatry, have found his books most helpful in their teaching and also in their work with patients. Unfortunately, we have not given enough emphasis to this subject in our teaching, but its relevance is attested to by the keen interest elicited immediately from medical students and trainees in psychiatry when the topic is mentioned. I use Dr. Jackson's writings in my teaching of medical students, psychiatric trainees, and theological students. His writings in this field still form the most complete and definitive body of work available today—in fact, the only work highly useful to both pastor and physician.

The hazards of unwisely managed grief have already been mentioned. Physicians, clergymen, and funeral directors should understand thoroughly the steps in the normal grief reaction—in which the work of mourning must be done, the bondage to the deceased broken, and new relationships formed. Where do we start in our effort to understand the proper management of the crisis of bereavement? We start with the rites and ceremonies surrounding death and dying. We must integrate our contemporary ways of dealing with death with the emotional needs of the survivors. Although the funeral is a rite for the dead, it is both socially useful and emotionally valuable for the living. The reorientation toward the funeral as a therapeutic ceremony is imperative. Such a ceremony is a link between the sacred, the bereaved, and the community.

For the purpose of illustrating the importance of the funeral, let us look closely at one part of it—the viewing of the body in the open casket—to show the healthiness of such a rite in meeting conscious and unconscious needs. Dr. Jackson discusses Erich Lindemann's psychiatric research, which has revealed that one of the common denominators in individuals with unresolved grief reactions is their inability to recall a clear picture of the deceased. The viewing of the body at the funeral would greatly aid in this recall.

Another common denominator Lindemann identified is the individual's unwillingness to face the pain of his bereavement. The funeral helps enforce reality, and the communal nature of the ceremony incorporates the community to share the pain with the bereaved.

The crisis of bereavement is faced at some time by every indi-

vidual. If he handles this crisis well, his health will not be jeop-
ardized. As Dr. Jackson points out, it is the misfortune of our
time that we expend great effort attacking our traditions and
ceremonials without understanding their usefulness to man
through the ages. Possibly some of the attacks themselves may be
born of the denial of grief or failure to do the work of mourning.

We are indeed grateful to Dr. Jackson for providing a stable
and experience-based approach to one of the most searching
psycho-theological problems of our time.

JAMES A. KNIGHT, B.D., M.D.,
Harkness Professor of Psychiatry
and Director of the Program in
Psychiatry and Religion,
Union Theological Seminary,
New York, N.Y. and
Lecturer on Psychiatry at
Cornell University Medical School

ONE

Sensible Open Discussion

Why this surge in talk about death and funerals?

When open discussion of any subject is long suppressed, a head of emotional steam builds up. Unless the pressure is relieved, an explosion will result.

For so long did we in America avoid or evade the consideration of death—including the work of the funeral director, the practice of embalming, and other elements of funeral practice —that a detonation was inevitable.

In late 1963, with the publication of Jessica Mitford's book, *The American Way of Death*, such an explosion occurred. Newspapers, magazines and television in turn began to give their attention to matters that had previously been discussed almost exclusively by physicians, clergymen, psychologists, psychiatrists, and funeral directors.

When any important part of life is obscured by hush-hush attitudes, or is beclouded with embarrassment, or has been misted over by anxiety, our ideas about it can be thrown grotesquely out of focus. Such is the situation in which many of us find ourselves today.

Now that the taboos have been broken through—now that the pent-up interest and curiosity can be satisfied—people want to make up for lost time.

Is this concentration on death healthy or morbid?

If ever we have an opportunity to correct one of the blanks in our way of looking at things, it is healthy. America went through something similar decades ago, when we believed it to be indelicate or even offensive to talk of birth or puberty. The language of the time was evasive and indirect. Instead of saying that a woman was pregnant, for example, one indicated that she was "indisposed" or was "knitting tiny garments."

We are now aware that in the absence of directness and honesty, half-truths and misconceptions are sometimes bred. America's attitudes toward sex grew confused, and for some the interest in the subject became morbid, not healthy.

The effects of this prudishness lingered on. Not until as late as World War II, for example, was the Surgeon General of the United States able to break through the veil of secrecy that had long existed about the subject of widespread venereal disease. He made a forthright statement about the social dangers of neglect and the need for wise and effective treatment. All of the evasiveness and subterfuge in the world would not heal one person, he pointed out; and the unwillingness to discuss the problems honestly had heretofore placed many innocent persons in danger. Only when the matter was out in the open could it be faced and could programs for social control and treatment be instituted.

I think it is morbid to repress discussion of any important subject that has to do with personal and community life. I deem it healthy indeed when free talk breaks into the clear.

What criticisms of current funeral practice have been made?

Those writers and commentators who have voiced criticisms of current funeral practices in America have raised one or more of these points: that the funeral practice they observe today frequently costs too much; that it provides an opportunity for unscrupulous businessmen to take advantage of painful emotions of the grief-stricken for personal gain; and that in return for their large money outlay, the bereaved get nothing that does them any good.

**What alternatives are suggested in place
of present practices?**

The alternatives that have most often been put forth are: that
interested adults organize themselves into memorial societies
which have as their purpose group negotiations with funeral
directors; that less expensive methods for disposal of the dead
be promoted; that modifications or eliminations be made in the
rites and ceremonies accompanying the disposal of the bodies;
and that bodies be donated for medical research or for student
training purposes in medical schools.

It is sometimes also suggested that careful consideration be
given to adopting practices employed in other countries—such
as France, where funerals are provided by the state, or England,
where simpler practices are general.

What is the real purpose of a funeral?

The funeral serves many major purposes. It provides an acceptable way for disposing of the body of a person who has died. And
it offers an opportunity for the expression of the religious faith
that can sustain the bereaved, the people who must face the loss
of one to whom they have been closely related emotionally.

Moreover, the funeral gives the community a chance to recognize the loss of one of its members, and in so doing to offer
support to the relatives of the dead person. This is usually a matter of both doing and saying.

To all who mourn, the funeral service provides an emotional
outlet for strong feelings, and an acceptable setting within which
to express them.

Who is involved in a funeral?

Not every funeral is the same, of course, and some involve a
great many more people than others. In the simplest funeral

there is the officiant, who conducts the religious service; the funeral director, who takes care of arrangements as to the body and the ceremony; the medical examiner, coroner, or physician, who fulfills the legal requirements of furnishing an authorization to bury or cremate the body; and then the members of the family, who participate in making the arrangements for the funeral, as well as neighbors and friends, who participate to a greater or lesser extent in the funeral activities, depending on circumstances.

A funeral for a person who held a prominent place in the life of the community may involve many more people. Sometimes fraternal organizations or special groups conduct their own services; police and fire department units, for example, may gather to show honor to one of their members. In some instances full military honors are accorded a member of the armed services who has died, or an honor guard or other military escort is provided.

How and why have funeral practices developed?

Wherever there is recorded history, there is a record of rites that honored or propitiated the dead. In some cultures the rituals were elaborate, such as those employed by the Egyptians; others were simple—for instance, those employed by some American Indian tribes. In any event, one mark of humanity has been the practice of burying the dead with ceremony.

Most social groups throughout history have developed ritualized acts to be performed by specific members of the group. Certain men and women in the community were chosen to carry out the ceremonial washing and preparation of the body for burial. We read in the New Testament of the woman who used rare and expensive ointment to prepare the body of Jesus for his burial. In early America a number of members of the community participated in the preparation of the dead for burial, some by the ritual of washing of the body, others by making the coffin, others by digging the grave.

The entire community then participated in the religious services that attended the burial of the dead. With the growth of communities, however, this practice changed. The need for coffins made it necessary for the cabinetmaker to specialize in his craft; similarly, individuals were called upon more and more often to perform the acts of preparation of the body for burial. Ultimately a group of persons emerged who became professionals in the community in that work.

Wherever they are observed, the purposes of funeral practices are essentially the same—to help the members of the community to face the full reality of the death of the one who has died, and to help the grieving to handle their own fears of death so that they can be better prepared to go on about the important tasks of living.

Do all cultures have the same funeral ceremonies?

While most cultures seem to have ceremonies designed to serve the same dual purposes—to show both the reality of death and the reality of continuing life—the variations in the forms of these ceremonies are almost endless. Some primitive cultures have evolved symbolic practices useful to them but so foreign to us as to be incomprehensible. On the other hand, our practices would fail to serve deep emotional needs of primitive people, and would therefore be unacceptable to them.

Even national traits and traditions have a strong bearing on funeral ceremonies, and one need only travel about our own country to observe ritualized acts quite different in their more obvious expressions. Some of the practices in Southern California would be unknown and unacceptable to many New Englanders, just as rites practiced with enthusiasm by some in New Orleans would be out of keeping in Minnesota, a state largely made up of people with a completely different background and religious tradition. Thus while almost all groups have as a common theme the showing of respect for the dead, their ceremonial acts are primarily in keeping with their own group standards and group needs.

What does a funeral have to do with the dignity of man?

The way various cultures treat the bodies of those who have died tends to reflect their philosophy as to the innate worth and dignity of man. In a society where the state is held to be more important than are the people who make it up, one often observes practices that show contempt for the rights and privileges we consider inalienable rights conferred upon man by his Creator.

This pattern of disregard threatens the whole idea of man's special quality as a spiritually-endowed being. When the body that has served as the physical residence of the spirit is treated with disrespect, the basic assumptions we cherish about life are challenged.

The care we show for the dead is really, then, a means we employ to guarantee respect for life. Indeed, what we are talking about here is a matter of the value we place upon life itself. If we make any part of man's experience cheap we cheapen all the rest of it. It is regrettably easier to downgrade respect for man's nature than to build it up again.

Thus we quite naturally and tenaciously cling to values that dignify man's innate qualities of being, and gaze with dismay on practices that would allow this basic respect to wither away.

The democratic quality of the funeral is generally recognized as respecting the good in man, avoiding judgments that man is ill-prepared to make on the total life of another, and laying away the remains with dignity and respect—trusting a divine justice to preserve the good with a wisdom we do not possess.

Then is the funeral for the dead or for the living?

When a person is dead he no longer has emotions or the capacity to express them. His worn-out body has neither thoughts nor the apparatus for thinking. The nerve mechanism that enabled him to care about his body ceases to function at the moment of death.

Anything that is done at the funeral or in the varied events that surround the ceremony can only be for those who survive and must continue to live on with their own thoughts, hopes, and apprehensions. If we could keep this fact always in mind, it would simplify much of our thinking about the meaning and value of funeral services. Funeral practices meet the personal, social, emotional and religious needs of those who continue to live.

TWO

The Nature of Grief

What major emotions are part of what we call grief?

Grief is a young widow who must seek a means to bring up her three children, alone. Grief is the angry reaction of a man so filled with shocked uncertainty and confusion that he strikes out at the nearest person. Grief is the little old lady who goes to the funeral of a stranger and cries her eyes out there; she is weeping now for herself, for an event she is sure will come, and for which she is trying to prepare herself.

Grief is a mother walking daily to a nearby cemetery to stand quietly and alone for a few moments before she goes on about the tasks of the day; she knows that part of her is in the cemetery, just as part of her is in her daily work. Grief is the deep sympathy one person has for another when he wants to do all he can to help resolve a tragic problem. Grief is the silent, knife-like terror and sadness that comes a hundred times a day, when you start to speak to someone who is no longer there. Grief is the emptiness that comes when you eat alone after eating with another for many years. Grief is teaching yourself somehow to go to bed without saying good night to the one who has died. Grief is the helpless wishing that things were different when you know they are not and never will be again. Grief is a whole cluster of adjustments, apprehensions and uncertainties that strike life in its forward progress and make it difficult to reorganize and re-direct the energies of life.

Grief is always more than sorrow. When doctors speak about "grief," they refer to the whole process that involves the person in adjusting to changed circumstances. They are referring to the deep fears of the mourner, to his prospects of loneliness, to the obstacles he must face as he finds a new way of living.

What are the roots of grief?

Grief is essentially a deprivation experience. We lose—or have taken from us—something that we cherished and do not want to give up.

It is strange how ill-prepared we often are for this, since our lives are so largely made up of deprivation experiences. Every time we make a choice we have to give up one alternative in order to take the other.

Death is the most acute form the deprivation experience can take. Not only do we lose what we love and cherish, but we also feel that some important part of our own being has been taken away in the act.

Because our sorrow is for a part of ourselves that seems to have been destroyed, we have a doubly difficult time in getting through the experience and on with the tasks of living. It is as with the amputee who "feels" pain in the limb he no longer has. His nerve system still wants to communicate with what was once there, even after that part of him is gone.

Our grief is rooted in emotions which reach out in all directions beyond our own physical being. Only as we literally pull up by the roots the feelings that no longer have a soil to sustain them are we able to let them take root again and be nurtured.

What is grief therapy?

"Grief" is the general word we use to describe the powerful set of emotions that permeate us when someone dearly loved dies. "Therapy" is the name given to a process that can help heal the deep hurts of grief.

Much of the current interest in helping the grieving person to handle these deep feelings wisely and well has grown out of the researches of Dr. Eric Lindemann of Harvard Medical School. As Professor of Psychiatry at Cambridge, he has done more research in the field of grief and its reactions on body, mind and spirit than has anyone else in the country. His findings on the wise management of grief have become basic to the work done by other psychiatrists and by psychologists, clergymen and funeral directors in helping those who suffer from acute grief to cope with their feelings effectively.

Is there any pattern to grief emotions?

The emotions that are a part of mourning usually take three different forms. Sorrow is the first of these. We mourn for the person who no longer is a part of our world; and at the same moment we mourn for ourselves, for our personal loss. We feel loneliness, emptiness, a painful sadness at having to face life without the person we have known so long and loved so deeply.

Another set of feelings clusters around our fears and anxiety. We are faced with sudden change. We are not sure what lies ahead. The fear of our own death lurks relentlessly in the back of our minds, and facing of the mystery of death always opens to us the gulf of the frightening unknown.

Another set of feelings has to do with very practical matters. We wonder what we are going to do next—where we will live, how we will pay our bills, how we will find for ourselves some security in a world that has suddenly changed so drastically. The future may seem threatening and uncertain. Sometimes we are required to make decisions by ourselves—decisions that were always shared before. This in itself may make us feel insecure and uncertain.

Emotions such as these usually come pouring in upon the life of a mourning person.

Is grief the same for persons of all ages?

Not at all. The grief of children, for instance, is usually seen in actions, not in words. When there has been a death in the family, the youngsters may suddenly become restless, irritable, perhaps even boisterous and noisy. Without realizing it, they may be seeking some way to calm their fears and loneliness. What they're doing is putting up a show—whistling in the dark, so to speak.

With persons who come out of a stolid, unemotional background, grief may be expressed quietly and over a long period. Those who come out of an emotionally volatile environment may have explosive expressions of grief that pass comparatively quickly.

With older people, grief is often expressed more in physical symptoms than in talk or action. When the aged speak among themselves, however, their conversations invariably dwell on death, illness and various catastrophes; it is as if, in talking about these things, they were getting some control over impending circumstances of life.

Middle-aged people often show their grief by changes in their personality and in the ways they do things. A widower may drive himself to work long hours, as if he could work his sorrow out of his system. Another man may lose all interest in his work, spending more and more time seeking emotional support in casual companionship. Sometimes the grieving person will take up the interests of the one whom he mourns, as if in so doing he can again share the life of the one he so acutely misses.

Grief shows itself in so many ways that it may be almost impossible to identify these acts and emotions for what they are.

What emotions in addition to sorrow do we show when someone dies?

Since grief is perhaps the most complex of emotions—and because its roots are so deep—the ways in which it shows itself are not only varied but may even on occasion be unrecognizable.

Sometimes the grief-stricken person will become oversensitive, embittered, and quickly moved to angry words and acts of fury. Reactions such as these are likely to puzzle and worry him; he may not realize that the anger he directs at family, friends and strangers is not an uncommon part of grief.

At other times a person may turn his anger toward himself. He will condemn himself for things he has said (or not said) and done (or not done) in the past. This is one of the ways he uses to give expression to feelings of guilt. ("Maybe," he says, "I could have prevented this!") His self-accusing emotion may lead to actions that serve as cruel self-punishment.

Sometimes the reaction to acute loss is utter despair. Life appears to have lost its meaning. Nothing seems to be worth the effort required to do it. To try to carry on without the love and companionship of the person who has died appears to be more of a burden than the mourner is willing to carry.

If this despair and the anger turned against the self persist over long periods of time, life can settle into a state of depression. Physicians and psychiatrists recognize the fact that "depression" is a damaging kind of mental, emotional illness.

Can minds go wrong when the shock of death is mishandled?

Yes, it appears that unwisely managed grief can be a precipitating factor in severe mental and emotional illness. Dr. Charles Anderson has reported in *The International Journal of Psy-*

choanalysis that nine per cent of the patients admitted to one English hospital were described as requiring treatment for "morbid grief reactions."

"For many years," declares Dr. Eric Lindemann, "psychiatrists and those interested in nervous breakdowns have talked about anxiety and about conflict as things that make people sick. It is only recently that we realize that depression, sorrow and loss of those who belong to the supportive human environment can be equally severe hazards in a person's life.

"In the wards of mental hospitals," continues Dr. Lindemann, "the patient's mental disease had very frequently broken out when some dear person had departed from his life."

**How do people show their anger when they are
filled with grief?**

Anger is a burningly strong emotion, and like most fiery emotions it tends to spread beyond the limits of controlled and reasoned actions.

When people are suffering from acute grief some of their feelings may show up in the form of anger. Part of the anger may be directed against God. The mourner may say, "If God took away the life of my dear one, then I will never have anything more to do with God as long as I live." In anger man denies any responsibility for the events that affect his own life and tries to place the blame on some remote source. The anger at God is sometimes directed at the minister who stands as a representative of religion. As one woman said to me, "If your God could kill a good man like my husband, you and your God are cheats and deceivers." I understood her feeling and was glad that she felt safe in venting some of her anger toward me.

Others turn their anger against the physician, blaming him for the unfortunate turn of events. Sometimes it is even a nurse who gets the blame. Quite often the funeral director gets more than his share of anger. Yet in any case it is not uncommon for those who make angry outbursts to write a letter a week or two later expressing deep appreciation for the services that were performed during a time of deep emotional stress.

The anger that shows up in incendiary words and irrational acts usually spends itself in safe boundaries. Indeed, it is less likely to cause later troubles than is anger that is repressed and turned against oneself in self-condemnation and guilt.

Is there any relationship between unwisely managed grief and juvenile delinquency?

In speaking of a dozen boys and girls whose lives exploded in violence, promiscuity and theft, Dr. Mervyn Shoor, psychiatrist in charge of the guidance clinic of Santa Clara's county juvenile probation department, said: "These were not children who hated. These are children who mourned." Then he explained how a death in the family can cause the kinds of anxiety and guilt that produce self-punishing behavior.

"Delinquent behavior by children and adolescents is sometimes a substitute grief reaction," he said. "These children were unable to release their feelings in socially acceptable ways when confronted with the impact of loss and death. They could not mourn normally; instead they masked their grief in delinquent behavior. Their mourning, then, was pathological."

The findings of Dr. Shoor verify an earlier study made by Dr. Rollo May of Columbia University, published under the title, *The Meaning of Anxiety*. In a careful study of the causes for the anti-social behavior of fourteen juvenile delinquents, Dr. May found that eleven of the fourteen had, during their early years, suffered the loss of a parent, or of one who had assumed the parental role. Their behavior later in life was the "acting out" of feelings of anger against what seemed to them an injustice: events that had deprived them of security and happiness.

While their acts were not reasoned actions, they were nonetheless an expression of emotional forces not easily understood or controlled. They were replying to sorrow with fury.

What does abnormal grief look like?

At close range it is difficult to separate the normal from the abnormal. Under the stress of powerful emotions, people say things and do things that are quite out of character.

We must ask ourselves, then, whether an act that may seem abnormal is part of a whole pattern of unusual actions and reactions or merely an isolated occurrence. And we want to see whether this new way of acting and reacting is becoming more firmly fixed or less so.

The abnormal usually shows up in extremes. Sometimes what we observe is a seeming inability to react emotionally at all. The person who is cold, efficient, impersonal, and dry-eyed under powerful emotional stress may be "under-reacting." The person who goes all to pieces may be "over-reacting." We cannot on the face of it say that the seemingly calm person is handling his situation well; neither can we say, in the face of an explosion of grief, that sorrow is shattering the other.

If the mourner has emotional weak spots in his nature, they may show themselves in aggravated form under the pressure of grief. Danger signals to watch for are unreasonable withdrawal from normal functions, excessive anger at others, or intense suspicion of others. These last may be directed against the physician, the minister, the funeral director or even toward members of the immediate family. Moods of inappropriate elation or deep depression may also be indications that things are not right.

One of the best ways to gauge abnormal emotional reactions is to observe a person and his behavior a month or so after the death has taken place. Most people will be quite back to normal by that time. If physical and emotional symptoms persist, and if the person is not able to function effectively after a few weeks, it is a fairly specific indication that he should have some special help in meeting his problems of readjustment.

What are the important steps in handling one's grief?

Since grief can lead to serious illness, it is vital that we handle and manage it rather than be dominated by it.

The wise management of grief calls for at least three important steps. First comes the painful task of facing the full reality of what has happened. Bluntly and with determination we must resist detours around the truth. We must realize that there is no known easy way to face the death of one who was deeply loved. We need courage to endure the pain, aware that ours is essentially a healthy pain, one that has within it its own healing qualities.

The second step centers around breaking some of the bonds that tie us to the person who has died. This is sometimes referred to as "withdrawing the emotional capital from the past" so that our feelings can be reinvested in the future. Life has been interrelated with the person who has died in many ways. A parent invests his hope in the life of a child. If the child dies he must withdraw the hope, for it is no longer valid. Only as he withdraws it can he look toward the future honestly. When an aged parent dies, adult children must recognize that they cannot have dependent feelings any longer. They must withdraw their dependence and declare their independence. Otherwise their lives will be perpetually bound to a false security.

Third, it is vital to develop ways that will make it possible for the person to find new interests, satisfactions and creative activities for the remainder of his life. New relationships must be formed, new acquaintances made. The energy of life will have to be planted in areas where it can be fruitful.

The past is past. While its memories may be treasured, one cannot live on memories alone and be healthy.

What is the best way to tell a person bad news?

There is no easy way to tell a person shattering news. There are, however, some guidelines that ought to be kept clearly in mind.

Whenever possible, the bearer of news should be face to face with the one who is to learn the distressing information, for then at least the bereaved will not be entirely alone in his ordeal. Even the one who brings the bad news is an ally in facing it.

The sad facts should be presented in as simple and direct form as possible. Beating around the bush only makes the process more painful.

The calm, direct approach does not add unnecessary anxiety to a problem that already has enough of its own. The person who brings the news should stand as part of the solution to the problem and not as another dimension to the problem itself. Anxiety and fear are easily communicated and amplified, but so also are calmness and confidence.

Having communicated the bad news, it is important to stand by to accept the emotional response and recognize both its importance and its validity. The first outpouring of feeling may be the important first step toward the acceptance of painful truth and the readjustment of life to it.

To sustain a person in these first painful moments is an important service that may produce good fruits for a long time to come.

How can a friend help a grieving person?

Much helpful counseling is done over the back fence as friend talks to friend without restraint about things that are important. In fact, there are times when an understanding neighbor can get closer to the real feelings of another person than can a minister, family doctor or psychiatrist.

One of the wisest things a good friend can do is to listen attentively. The effort to pour out our painful feelings often relieves emotional pressures more effectively than anything else. To have someone who is ready and willing to be a sympathetic and understanding listener is especially important at the time when grief is most intense. This is not a time for friends to compare tragedies or to play "Can you top this?" It is a time for perceptive, responsive listening.

In addition to listening to what your friend has to say, it is also important to receive his injured and shattered feelings with attitudes that make these feelings seem proper and right. Sometimes a shoulder to cry on is a most important part of the ventilating of deep feelings. To know that someone is willing to feel with you even when you cannot express your feelings very well is important. And this is often more vital a week or two after the funeral than it is during the time when many people are around.

Is crying helpful in expressing one's grief?

From early childhood the use of the tear glands as a form of expressing deep feelings is a part of life. As we grow older we may not cry as often as we did when we were children, but when strong emotions need to be expressed it is a useful thing to have these safety valves in good working order.

Dr. Gert Heilbrunn, in an article titled "On Weeping" in *The Psychoanalytic Quarterly*, wrote in 1955, "Whenever stimuli of grief, disappointment, anger, or 'overwhelming' joy exceed the tolerance of the organism, the ensuing state of tension is alleviated by a release of energy from various organs or organ systems which abolishes the tension. The shedding of tears furthers the homeostatic principle so well that it is the favorite mechanism of release during childhood. Probably it would so continue throughout life were it not suppressed by the demand of society for emotional restraint and replaced by other modes of discharge."

The opinion of psychiatrists appears to be that crying can be a healthy and useful way of discharging pent-up emotions. When one is faced with so powerful an emotion as grief, weeping is singularly appropriate and helpful. We should not be afraid to cry. We should recognize that others have the right to cry if and when they want to.

How can one help himself when he is suffering from acute grief?

I have observed that in helping others we clarify things for ourselves. Years ago my oldest son died as the result of a tragic accident. I have since found that my efforts to help other people face their grief and comprehend its meaning has somehow assisted me—not only in handling my own emotions, but also by giving me the feeling that what I am doing serves as a living memorial for the one I loved. My effort to make sure that even in his dying there is a continuing creative element manifests itself in a ministry to others.

One of the things a person who is suffering from grief must do is to be kind to himself. Often we are our own harshest critics, judges and juries. We say and do things to ourselves that we would bitterly resent were others doing it to us. It is mandatory that we stand off and look at ourselves, our motives and the events of our lives as if we wanted to be our own good friend rather than our own severe accuser.

It is also helpful for us to try to look at events and feelings from the point of view of the person who has died. Only then can we begin to modify our judgments and reactions in the light of what the understanding love of the dead person might have been were he present to give us the advantage of his counsel and insight.

**Is there evidence that grief can cause more
than mental anguish?**

Yes. Dr. Lawrence LeShan has pointed out that the "bleak and
utter despair" which often accompanies the loss of someone
dearly loved appears to be a factor in bringing about chemical
changes within the body.

Indeed, researches in psychosomatic medicine are revealing
insights into the relationship between acute and chronic grief
and the development of malignant tissue. In an article in *The
Journal of the National Cancer Institute,* Dr. LeShan quotes the
findings of Dr. Willard Parker, who summed up his fifty-three
years of surgical experience with cancer in these words: "It is a
fact that grief is especially associated with the disease."

Dr. LeShan indicates the connection between cancer and
grief by stating that emotions affect the glandular system most
immediately. The glandular system controls body chemistry, and
body chemistry controls cell division. When the chronic disturbance of the emotions that can come from unwisely managed
grief keeps the glandular system disturbed, the result is a persistent disturbance of the body chemistry, and this could be a
cause of irregular and unhealthy cell division.

There appears to be clear evidence that unwisely managed
grief could be a significant factor in physical as well as mental
ills. This is yet another reason for deep interest in grief by all
who work constantly with mourners—psychiatrists and clergymen, funeral directors and psychologists, internists and patho-
logists, social workers and guidance counselors.

How long should grief last?

The most distressing physical symptoms of grief—weakness,
nausea, faintness, disorientation and generalized discomfort
—should pass rather quickly, usually in a day or two.

The inclination to weep continually, the uneasy discomfort when in the presence of other people, and the desire to get off by oneself may last for several days.

All these expressions of grief should have disappeared in four or five weeks, although sorrow itself will remain. A temporary desire for solitude at all costs is one thing; it is a mood that will occasionally recur with fresh reminders of one's grief. An almost permanent desire to be alone to brood and despair is another thing—not an emotion but a symptom.

If the bereaved finds it difficult to sleep, to do his work or to handle the routine activities of life after a month or so, it would be wise to talk with a physician, clergyman or psychiatrist about the problems of readjustment.

How is grief relieved?

Grief is relieved by time, by understanding and by the ongoing creative impulses of life itself.

When sorrow comes, the days drag. The long hours of these slow-moving days are weighted with pain and defeat. But all people in all places have recognized that time has about itself a healing quality. As time moves on, things that were out of perspective begin to move back into their proper place.

When we understand what is happening it is easier to bear it. It is meaningless suffering that is unendurable. When we can grasp the fact that death is part of the cycle of life, then death in general is not so distressing; rather it is the individual death which we contemplate that presents the problem to us. But if the individual death is related to the divine process, we are then able to see it in the larger perspective that understanding adds to the slow wisdom of time.

Life has about itself a certain built-in momentum. It shows up in the meeting of problems and in the finding of solutions. The effort to do the next thing that must be done helps us to relieve the generalized feelings of our grief.

So we go on about the tasks of the day, and the days lengthen into weeks and soon, without our being aware of what has happened, the deep wounds slowly begin to heal and even the scar tissue begins to fade away. Life will never again be quite the same as it was, but there is still life to be lived and it still can be good.

THREE

The Funeral and Grief

Why are social ceremonies important?

Ceremonies are usually elaborate ways of doing things that really don't have to be done at all except to satisfy important emotional needs.

You can get a diploma without attending elaborate commencement exercises, but nonetheless "graduation days" are wonderful occasions that mark important milestones in life.

A man and woman can be just as legally married by obtaining a license and having a justice of the peace mutter a few words, yet few people are satisfied with that. They choose instead to spend hundreds or even thousands of dollars that might otherwise be invested or used for furnishing the home to have a big wedding with many friends in attendance, a gay reception with an expensive dinner and flowers, gowns, and much, much more. They take pictures of it so that they will never forget this wonderful moment. None of this wedding ceremony is legally necessary, but it serves an important purpose in the lives of the participants. They seek to surround a most important event in their life with all the meaning, dignity, tradition and joy they can employ.

Actually, as with most ceremonies, it is an investment in meaning, perhaps difficult to justify in terms of hard dollars and cents, yet so important to the emotional needs of man that wherever you find civilized persons you find elaborate ceremonies, made lavish with an extravagance that reason alone won't easily justify. It may be the crowning of an English monarch with great pomp and ceremony, or it may be the baptism

of a little baby with quiet joy; the meaning of the social ceremony has its value not in what it costs but in what it does for
people.

What do healthy ceremonials do for people?

Healthy ceremonials are worthy of such a classification when
they serve a useful, healthful purpose for a majority of the normal persons in any given community.

A healthy ceremonial is one that provides an appropriate setting in which people can easily express legitimate feelings relating to important events in their lives or in the life of the group.

A funeral will serve as a healthy ceremonial when it helps
the individuals in a community accept rather than deny their far-
reaching feelings; moreover, it serves healthful ends when it is
conducted in an atmosphere that permits facing reality not only
personally but socially. When a number of other people accept
a fact, it is increasingly difficult for one or two members of the
group to deny it.

The healthy ceremonial can make it possible for the group to
verify its faith in the future by saying, in effect, "We know what
is happening to you, for we have been through it ourselves. We
also know that you can handle the crisis and meet the future, for
we ourselves have been able to do so. Our presence here
is verification of your ability to find your way through even so
devastating an experience as this."

The ceremonial depends for its efficacy not so much on what
is said as it does on the group expression of its own experiences,
and on the recognized, ritualized expressions of faith and feeling. While such expressions may vary widely, their meaning is
almost universally understood and accepted.

This ability to communicate thought and feeling through
acts that are commonly understood gives to the ceremonial its
special value.

What do unhealthy ceremonials do to people?

Unhealthy people tend to develop for themselves unhealthy ceremonial expressions. Men with an unhealthy streak of cruelty encourage cockfights. Those with an unhealthy compulsion for gambling see nothing wrong with widespread playing of dice and roulette. While these two forms of behavior may not seem like ceremonials at first, they serve that purpose for the persons who use them.

Ceremonials may be used to build detours around reality, just as they can be developed to help people face reality. Gambling, for example, requires adult men and women to believe something patently unreal—that one can "will" dice to fall in a certain way, or that one's personal wishes can make a horse run faster or a little clay ball fall into one slot instead of another.

Those who do not want to face the full reality of death may develop ceremonials that make it unnecessary for them to look at death. Insofar as these ceremonials are escapes, they tend to be unhealthy expressions.

Similarly, people with morbid curiosity and abnormal apprehensions concerning death may try to satisfy their pathological needs through excesses in the other direction.

It is important to realize that the reaction to a ceremonial is a highly individual and personal thing. In the final analysis, ceremonials must be judged on how they help the people involved to fulfill their important emotional needs.

What do physicians and psychiatrists say about the needs and values of traditional funeral practice in America?

We have begun to see some of the psychological imperatives of the funeral for the mourners. It has as its first task the frank facing of painful reality. Second, it must help the living realize that they are now separated not only physically but in their dependency emotions as well from the one who has died. Third, it must set the living in the direction of life, not death.

Dr. Eric Lindemann, the nation's leading authority on grief, speaks as both a physician and psychiatrist when he describes the needs of the bereaved as follows:

"Religious agencies have led in dealing with the bereaved. They have provided comfort by giving the backing of dogma to the patient's wish for continued interaction with the deceased, have developed rituals which maintain the patient's interaction with others, and have counteracted the morbid guilt feelings of the patient by Divine Grace and by promising an opportunity for 'making up' to the deceased at the time of a later reunion. While these measures have helped countless mourners, comfort alone does not provide adequate assistance in the patient's grief work. He has accepted the pain of his bereavement. He has to review his relationships with the deceased, and has to become acquainted with the alterations in his own modes of emotional reaction. His fear of insanity, his fear of accepting the surprising changes of his feelings, especially the overflow of hostility, have to be worked through. . . . He will have to find an acceptable formulation of his future relationship to the deceased. He will have to verbalize his feelings of guilt, and he will have to find persons around him whom he can use as 'primers' for the acquisition of new patterns of conduct."

The religious and community acts that are part of the funeral practice become the means through which some of these needs, as described by Dr. Lindemann, can be met. They are a mechanism which the personality uses in coping with severe emotional problems. Thus we see that the events surrounding our rituals and ceremonies for the dead are, in truth, rituals and ceremonies for the living.

How important is a clear image of the dead person?

Dr. Lindemann has pointed out two major conditions peculiar to those who suffer mental and emotional disturbances as a result of unwisely managed grief. "One of them is that the person in many of these states cannot remember very well the image of the deceased." The distress that comes with fears of viewing the dead body is such that the person will avoid doing it. Yet in avoiding the act he makes so vast an emotional effort that he may completely obliterate the memory picture of the dead person.

"Not being able to remember the image of the deceased, he puts it out of his mind, which is somewhat convenient in the beginning," Dr. Lindemann declares. "It saves suffering, and the suffering is avoided by a good many people because mourning belongs to the most painful state that human beings know." But to put the memory or the visual image of the person mourned out of mind at the cost of one's mental health is too great a price to pay to avoid momentary suffering. It is far better to fix the image clearly in one's mind, perhaps by standing quietly beside the casket in the funeral home hour after hour, until the full emotional meaning of the death is grasped. Then, with the memory image clearly in mind, the work of reorganizing deep feelings can take place in an orderly manner.

This clear image of the dead person becomes the working basis from which reorganization of life takes place. When the image is not clear and the deceased is put out of mind, the mourner may begin to create illusory pictures that serve ill as a foundation for rebuilding a life.

What do we mean when we speak of "body image"?

Everyone is aware of his own body. Its state of health is perhaps the most important thing in the world to each individual. Psychologists know that we all build up a whole bundle of feelings about our own bodies, and this they call "body consciousness." Through his own body consciousness an individual is able to imagine what other people are feeling even when nothing is happening to him. You can imagine the unpleasantness of a tooth extraction even if your own teeth are in splendid condition. In this way our own body image is projected out toward other people.

In our culture we are quite body conscious, and our absorption with the state of our bodies shows itself in two ways, "body denial" and "body fulfillment." Many things we do are acts of body denial, where we say in effect that we do not like this part or that part of having a body. When we shave in the morning or apply a deodorant, we practice body denial. When we enjoy a good meal and stretch ourselves with delight, we are engaging in body fulfillment.

Part of our projected body image is an unconscious movement ahead in time. For instance, we can't really accept the fact that our bodies will die—or that the bodies of other people will die, either. So when we think of cremation or dissection we can almost cringe at the thought of the heat or the sharp knife. Our imagination, our body image and our body function are all tied together.

When we think of the death of someone else, part of our body image—with all its special feelings—is attached to his body. We tend to feel sensations he is now incapable of feeling. We know this doesn't make sense, of course, but we also know it happens. We learn to accept the fact that some emotions are outside the sphere of the logical and rational.

In the process of working through grief, the feelings that go with the body image are part of the problem. They must be understood. Their sensitivities must be taken into account. So we try not to do things to a dead body that would stimulate strong reactions relating to our own body image. Thus the respect for a dead body in funeral ceremonials is a way of protecting the body image of the living from intolerable injury.

Why do we try to avoid looking at death?

There is something threatening about looking into the face of death. I have often been in the hospital, at the bedside of a mortally sick person, when the last flicker of life faded away. Almost immediately the nurse or physician in attendance picked up the sheet and covered the face of the man or woman who had died just seconds before. It was somewhat as if they were saying, "This is something we cannot bear to look at."

But why? Is it because the person who died is worse off? That we do not know, although we do know that his time of physical suffering is past. Perhaps the explanation is that his death is a reminder of our own mortality, and that this is a fact we do not usually want to acknowledge.

"One can no more look steadily at death than at the sun," said La Rochefoucauld, the French sage. Yet even a lifetime devoted to avoiding the reality of death would not make it possible for us actually to avoid it or its meaning for our lives.

Thus when we would "look away," we need the firm but friendly urging that denies the escape and faces the reality. One of the benefits of funeral service is that it makes it possible for us to face this reality without gruesomeness.

In facing the fact of death we make more mature our own adjustment to life and its limits. Evans Carlson, the commanding officer of Carlson's Marine Raiders, once said to me, "Anyone who is afraid to die does not deserve to live." This seems like a blunt and perhaps terrifying statement. But think about it for a while, and you may come to see that it puts a large truth in a few words.

Do people often try to deny the reality of death?

Yes, I think we have all seen this occur many times. When someone is called on the telephone with news of the death of a close friend, a typical first response is one of denial. "No. Oh, no. It can't be true." The speaker knows, as well as anyone else, that it can be true, and that sooner or later it will be true for every one of us. And yet the first impulse is to resist and deny the uncomfortable truth.

As a chaplain with the Air Force during World War II, I saw denial on the part of parents who had received the fateful telegram from the War Department. It was my duty to visit families of servicemen in my particular unit who died. Again and again I found the relatives denying reality and clinging to illusion. This they expressed by saying to me, "I know about the telegram and all that, but nothing can keep me from believing that some day the door will open and our son will come in and say, 'I was captured by the enemy and it has taken me all this time to get out.'" At other times they talked about the possibility of amnesia, or of his being shot down in a remote region. In each instance this was a carefully constructed denial which they chose to cling to rather than accept the painful truth. It was a flimsy basis on which to build their response to the future, and yet they could not really begin to reorganize their living until they were willing to accept the facts.

Some of the services in vogue today seem to be designed more to deny reality and fact than to reënforce the truth that must be courageously accepted.

Why is an inadequate view of death dangerous?

An inadequate view of death usually leads to an inadequate view of life. When that happens, life can be abused—and sometimes even destroyed. Let me show you how this can happen.

People who have deep and unresolved fears of death may

try to prove to themselves that they are not really so frightened. They may make light talk about the subject, joking about graveyards, funeral directors and serious disease. They may even participate in games designed to prove that they have no fear of death.

One game of this kind is played by teen-agers who race toward each other in their cars to see which one will pull out first and thus be "chicken." This game is a variation of "Russian roulette," in which one live bullet is put in the chamber of a revolver. The chamber is then spun and the trigger pulled as the weapon is aimed at one's own head. Such a gamble with life could only be taken by one who was trying to say, "See—I am not really afraid of death." But the real tragedy is that a person who does such things is actually saying that life means so little to him that he would make a plaything out of it. Certainly that is a tragically inadequate view of life.

Variations on this demeaning philosophy show up in other ways—for instance, when a person commits suicide with the strange twist of logic that makes him feel that in this way he is cheating death by controlling it in time and place. The daredevil, the person who deliberately seeks the most dangerous kind of work, and the person who takes unnecessary chances in life are often people trying to prove to themselves that they do not fear death.

Actually what they are doing is quite the reverse. For them, death is an unhealthy preoccupation that affects every aspect of their living.

Why do people get so emotionally upset when the subject of death is raised?

This question assumes a universal response that I do not believe to be invariably true. Mature men and women, whose philosophy of life and death is well developed, can think and talk about death quite casually and without personal apprehension.

It is quite true, however, that for many of us the whole subject is fraught with anxiety and discomfort. This may be caused by a number of things. Sometimes it is caused by childhood experiences, when death was not talked about and so became especially distressing to contemplate. For others the mention of death may immediately recall one particular death that was so emotionally damaging that it has never quite been accepted. For instance, a car driven by a friend of mine struck and killed a woman who stepped out from between two parked cars. He was unable to avoid the accident, and this fact was established without question by a court that investigated the accident. Yet even now, many years later, the mention of death still triggers memories for my friend of that horrible moment when he saw what was happening and was helpless to do anything about it.

Almost generally the mention of death also reminds one of his own sure fate, and this is in itself quite distressing for people who have not developed any understanding of the meaning of their own existence. Dr. Herman Feifel has found in his research work that most people over fifty have as a major preoccupation the thought of their own death. To think about death when one is not sure of the meaning of life is bound to be upsetting.

What happens when many deaths occur not in homes but in hospitals?

A college president in New England said recently that most of the students in his college had never had a personal encounter with death. A century ago that would not have been true. In yesterday's large households, sheltering as they so often did several generations and many relatives, there was a persistent process of birth and death. The life cycle was intimately known. The members of a household lived close to elemental things.

Now, however, death is usually a thing of the hospital, the battlefield or the highway. Those who care for the dying are professionally trained for their tasks, and are usually not related to or even previously acquainted with the dying person. This means that the one who is dying feels separated from those who have sustained his life and who really know him. Similar emotions of being "cut off" afflict the next of kin of the dying person. They have, in essence, given over their special interest to others who cannot really share it.

Separated from the dying person in his most critical hours, they tend to harbor the attitude that what is happening is not really so and will not take place. When the doctor comes into the hospital waiting room and says, "I must tell you that your father has just expired," those who listen hear and understand the words, but the deeper meanings are much slower in arriving. The relatives need to have affirmed for their consciousness in ways that cannot be misunderstood the full meaning of what has happened. Often this awareness comes to them not at the hospital but at a funeral home, where the slow but sure recognition of the truth reaches those who haven't before been able to accept the facts that are so painful.

What should children be told about death?

Death is very much a part of the child's world. He sees death on television, in magazines and in books. He cannot be shielded from its existence. Yet he can have its meaning interpreted for him skillfully, so that he grows to understand what death means rather than to dwell in morbid fear of it.

With that in mind it is important to remember that children live more in feelings than in reasoned actions. If strong feelings are let loose in the family, the child is aware of them. He then becomes especially concerned about the answers to his questions. A child should never be lied to, for he quickly senses a lie, and is then doubly troubled. He not only fails to get the answers he needs, but he also feels threatened if the adults upon whom he depends for security fail him by lying. He may next wonder if they have ever told him the truth about anything.

In answering the questions children ask it is important to know exactly what they are asking. Usually their questions are quite simple and factual, and it is unnecessary to over-answer them by trying to attach adult meanings to the child's query.

No child should ever be forced to go to a funeral home, but if he wants to go he should be accompanied by a competent adult who can answer his questions and make him feel that he is in the presence of a natural phenomenon that affects all of life sooner or later. It is usually better if young children go to the funeral home when no service is going on. In this way they can be told about death in their own terms and be free of anxiety, unsatisfied curiosity and morbid fears. Some youngsters carry into their early teens a form of death denial, the belief that the one being buried is actually still alive. This common worry is eased by the viewing of the remains of the parent, brother or sister who has died, and by other aspects of the ceremony.

FOUR

The Question of Funeral Services

Isn't it good to try to remove pain and discomfort from life?

In answering this question we must recognize that there are different kinds of pain. Some we would gladly remove; some we must hold on to as valuable.

For instance, we would generally agree that it is a good thing to remove the physical pain that goes along with a dental extraction or a surgical operation. Here the function of pain as a danger signal has served its purpose. Now a competent professional person can remove the source of the pain without danger to the organism. Pain teaches us, warns us, and guides us in many ways that help us keep our bodies healthful and intact. Without them we could easily be cut, burned, frozen, or poisoned.

There are emotional pains, however, that cannot be removed without hazard. For instance, it is not a comfortable thing to suffer from a guilty conscience. Yet if we did not experience the dismay that comes with guilt feelings, we would not know the meaning of moral choices. And if we had no basis for moral choices, our whole structure of society would fall apart. No one of us would be able to depend on anyone else. Moral responsibility can never be separated from the discomfort that comes with feelings of guilt.

So also our feelings of grief tend to show not only the value we have placed upon the life of the person we mourn, but also demonstrate the value we place upon life in general. To try to blot out that discomfort would be to threaten the whole structure of human values. Some pain is so valuable for personal and social good that we cannot blot it out without doing incalculable harm.

Should a funeral service be planned to "make things easy" for the mourners?

Here we meet with a conflicting set of purposes. We recognize that there is no easy way of facing the death of one who was important to our structure of life. It is painful—perhaps the most poignant pain that humans experience.

Naturally we want to ease the pain in any way we can. One way to do so is by showing compassion, patience, consideration, understanding and kindness. But this is quite different from an effort to "make things easy" by denying strong feelings and by trying to prevent their expression.

We will discuss some of the ways in which misguided people try to "make things easier." They attempt to avoid any show of sorrow by the mourners—weeping, moaning, sobbing. They seek to hide the hurt by masking it with drugs. They try to hide the loss—by hiding the body, by cloaking emotion, by suggesting a hasty trip that will remove the mourner from the scene of his loss. Death is an amputation; concealment will not change the fact. It will only delay and therefore distort reality.

Should people take sedatives when someone dies?

In our culture we have developed the art of taking the pain out of many uncomfortable circumstances. We employ anaesthetics for surgery and childbirth. We request a shot of novocaine when we have a tooth pulled. We develop the assumption that there is something we can swallow to relieve every painful experience.

But the pains that afflict our physical mechanism are different from those that sting and bruise and batter our minds and emotions. We cannot build byways around those pains or mask them for long; only by coping with them directly and quickly can we reduce the hurt.

Dr. Paul Hoch, mental health commissioner for the State of New York, cautions against the indiscriminate use of sedation when dealing with emotional crises. While the use of sedatives involves the strategy "of knocking out the anxiety-mediating neural mechanisms . . . it can be rightly pointed out that these measures are not psychotherapy." Actually they only delay the readjustments that have to be made, often unfortunately postponing them until a later date. Consider the common case of a woman left alone when her husband dies. During the few days when friends gather around her, she uses sedation to delay the truth of her lonely, frightening situation. Then when her friends are gone and the impact of her new aloneness is at its most shattering, she ceases using sedation; now, defenseless and without the support of others, she must face reality at last. All that she has done is to postpone her healthy feelings and their healthy expression until a more difficult time.

Nature has a wisdom of its own which helps the person to tolerate discomfort at a schedule the emotions set for themselves. To interfere with this natural process upsets nature's own wisdom, creating new problems rather than solving existing ones. Only in extreme cases, where a person is already under medical supervision, should this practice of sedation for grief be approved.

What about drinking alcohol in excess during the mourning period?

Alcohol is a form of sedation. In its molecular structure, it is much the same as ether and chloroform. The main difference is that ether and chloroform are absorbed into the body through the lungs, while alcohol is more slowly absorbed through the tissues that line the alimentary canal. The anaesthetics which are inhaled are administered carefully by skilled specialists, but alcohol is usually self-administered. The immediate effects tend nonetheless to be comparable. There is a temporary blotting-out of pain. There is no solving of the problem, however, just as there is no curing of an ailment with sedatives.

All that is accomplished in any case is postponement in the facing of the problem. In acute grief, such postponement is unwise; it can become a chronic device to keep the bereaved from facing reality.

With alcohol there is another aspect that needs to be considered. Alcohol is also a depressant, and one of the major emotional dangers that comes with grief is a state of depression that sometimes accompanies the acute loss. To administer any form of drug that aggravates the danger of depression is unwise and even emotionally dangerous.

There are some pains that are best taken straight, and the pains that go with grief are of this sort. There is no quick and easy way of getting around them. When one tries to do so he merely fools himself, for if he is going to emerge from his despair he must face the realities openly. And the sooner he does so, the better.

How effective is a funeral service without a body?

The presence of the body makes the funeral service specific. It clearly becomes a service for the person who is there represented by his remains. When the body is not present, the service tends to become very much like other services conducted in the church, and thereupon loses much of its meaning.

A funeral service without a body present is usually called a memorial service. It may well be a beautiful and inspiring service, as any church service should be, but it is almost certain to lack specific reference to the individual to whom honor is being paid. The unique thing about any funeral service is the fact that a clearly identifiable person recently was among us and now is not.

People who have attended memorial services sometimes say, "It just didn't seem like a funeral." If the purposes of a funeral are to be served, then a funeral service with its unique characteristics is necessary. A funeral without the body present is somewhat like a baptism or marriage by proxy, or a birthday celebration without the birthday child there. The ceremony can be carried out, but it lacks individual identity.

Should a dead body be looked at?

Only abnormal interests are served, I think, when one is impelled to look at a dead body merely out of morbid curiosity. But for close relatives and dear friends, the viewing of a body can be a vital part of coming to terms with reality. A sorrowing look into the face of death confirms the truth of what has happened—truth that our minds and hearts desperately wish not to accept. Indeed, this moment often starts the process we call "wise grief management."

It is at this point that we might well reëxamine some of the practices that are employed in various parts of our country. The whole idea of having a casket open in church when once the religious service has begun—or even during a religious service conducted in the funeral home—violates the purpose of the religious service. The goal of that service is to direct the mind beyond the physical to the spiritual. Thus I would recommend that the casket be closed with private prayer in the presence of the immediate family before the religious service begins, and that it not be opened again. The important psychological values served by seeing the dead body are fully satisfied by viewing before the religious service. The importance of this is usually for the immediate family and for friends who have strong emotional ties to the person who has died.

Isn't viewing the body "too painful" and "barbaric"?

There is no doubt that the act of looking at the dead body of one who has been loved can be painful. Often the pain is more in the dread of doing than in the actual viewing.

It is this accumulation of dread which must be dealt with, for it can be carried into the future. The choice is not between a painful act and a painless act. The pain exists. It is a fact. We decide only how we will deal with it—whether we will handle the pain as a sharp, clean stabbing of the consciousness, or whether we will carry a smoldering, festering injury that will infect our whole consciousness increasingly as time moves on.

There is certainly nothing barbaric about facing life or death with complete openness and honesty. It may be that in subtle efforts to keep from being what we call "barbaric" we come closest to the ruthless abuse of our own feelings and those of others.

What do you think of the open casket type of service?

As I have already stated, I think the practice of having the casket open during the religious service is inappropriate, and to be discouraged.

The religious service for the dead is designed to direct thoughts and feelings toward the spiritual realities that can sustain the spirit of men in the crises of life. To try to present these spiritual values when the attention of people is fixed on an outworn body that is about to be interred or cremated is a violation of the purpose of the religious service.

To have the religious service end and then have the casket opened so that the congregation can perform the rite of filing past the casket is an inexcusable violation of the intent and purpose of the religious service.

The important psychological benefits of viewing the body can be satisfied before the time the religious service begins.

What good does embalming do?

Embalming doesn't do the person who has died any good. It has no purpose at all as far as any value to the deceased is concerned.

The value of embalming lies in the fact that it makes it possible to delay the natural processes of decomposition so that psychologically and socially suitable funeral ceremonies can be carried through. In our day, when members of a family may be scattered to the far parts of the country, with some even residing abroad, it is often necessary to allow three or four days for the family to gather before services are conducted. It would be difficult to conduct a funeral ceremony that served a useful psychological and spiritual purpose in the presence of a body that had not been embalmed so as to retard temporarily the decomposition that follows death.

Except when death has been caused by certain diseases, there are in most instances no legal requirements that make embalming necessary. However, when a body is to be transported, embalming is required by law. And when there is not immediate interment or cremation, embalming is required by law in most states after the expiration of a certain number of hours after death. Embalming is also the means to restore to an earlier appearance the body of one whose death is particularly hard to accept because it was sudden and violent, or because devastating illness was cruelly disfiguring.

The important reasons for embalming have to do with concern for the living, not for the dead.

What about putting make-up and cosmetics on a dead body?

When a body is prepared for the funeral service, an effort is made to recreate a resemblance to the appearance the person had while alive. Proper respect for the body determines that it should not be made ready for viewing in an unkempt and disheveled condition. So the hair is combed and the face shaved.

Sometimes the comment is made that the dead body looks "years younger" than the person did when he died. With death there is sometimes a relaxation of face muscles, and the worried, pain-ridden countenance falls into easy, relaxed lines. This often produces changes that the family observes but for which the funeral director has no responsibility.

It is no secret that in our culture many people try to improve on the achievements of nature by special cosmetics applied to their faces. This has become more natural than unnatural in our culture. We often hear women say, "I can't go yet—I don't even have my face on." Naturally they are not speaking of the face nature gave them, but of the improvements in color and design they want to make on nature.

Since the efforts to prepare the body for viewing take into account the appearance of the person while he lived, it is quite natural that the modified appearance cosmetics provide would also have to be considered. What is objectionable to many of us is the occasional inappropriate use of make-up. This might happen when the funeral director did not know the deceased well enough to do an accurate recreation of his appearance. Then he may create an appearance that needs to be corrected under the supervision of the family.

Do you think all new clothes should be put on a dead body?

The practice that is almost universal in America today is for the person who has died to be buried in a favorite suit or dress. Often when I have sat in with a family while funeral arrangements were being made, I have heard the funeral director ask the family if they would provide him with the clothes they would like to see on the deceased.

However, there are some people in America who come out of a religious and cultural background which believes that part of the preparation of the body for burial requires that it be clothed in all new garments. The funeral director then is expected to furnish as part of his service a complete set of new clothes. But here again, it should be kept in mind that the new clothes are not really for the corpse, which has no way of being aware of them, but are rather for the family, which is expressing its belief as to what is right and proper in relation to the one who has died.

There are, of course, those who, because of where they live or what they do for a living, do not have clothing deemed suitable by their family for burial. Therefore, those responsible for the funeral purchase such clothing either from a clothing or department store or from the funeral director.

Should the remains be laid out with glasses on?

It is quite obvious that putting glasses on a dead body serves no purpose as far as the body is concerned. Its eyes do not see and never will again.

The practice of putting glasses on the dead body is primarily so that the familiar image of the person will be reënforced. Then there will be for the viewers a fuller consciousness of the fact of death, and of the clear and unmistakable identity of the one who has died. This is the essential first step in sound grief management. To use a comparison, we might say that it is foolish to place dentures in the mouth of the dead person because he will never eat again. The only purpose for using dentures is to give a more recognizable appearance to the face.

The important functions of clear identity, acceptance of reality, and adjustment to it all require that there be as few means for escape into the unreal as possible. When a family stands by the casket and says, "That doesn't look like John," they are in effect saying that what has happened isn't real. This may be a trick of the mind to avoid facing the painful aspects of grief. If, on the other hand, they say, "John looks so natural," they are saying that they cannot deny what they see, and are trying to come to terms with it.

What about terminology in funeral practice?

Whenever language becomes less open and honest and more evasive and devious, it becomes part of the conspiracy to avoid facing circumstances as they are. To call the room where the body lies a "slumber room" is to participate in a deception pretending that the dead person is merely asleep.

To call the remains by a surname seems strangely inappropriate. When Wendell Willkie died, a radio commentator reported on the passage of the funeral cortege. He told of the solemn processional, using such phrases as "Now Mr. Willkie is turning into Fifth Avenue" or "Now Mr. Willkie is being taken into the door of the church."

A clergyman wrote a letter to *The New York Times* to point out that it was about time that we recognized the difference between a dead body and the person who once inhabited it. Quite properly it could be said, "Mr. Willkie's remains are now being taken through the door of the church." The right use of language could do much to clarify the relationships that exist between life and death and so could serve the purpose of wise grief management.

Let us learn to say "The body of Mrs. Smith is in this room," or "The physical remains of Mr. Jones will be buried at Greenwood Cemetery." Such phrases as "he has passed on," or "he has gone to his reward," or "he will be laid to rest" leave much to be desired in open honest communication. Let us use language as it was intended to be used—to communicate thought, meaning and feeling, rather than to use it to obscure, confuse and deny.

What about the dangers of language that is afraid to say what is means?

Very often we use language to keep from saying something rather than to say it. This is often the case when we feel that words will trigger painful feelings. Then we sometimes use words that we hopefully believe will be less painful. In the long run we only make the problem worse by our inability to face the truth about ourselves and our experiences.

This practice is quite general in our culture. I picked up a dental student's magazine recently and learned in it that there are some words which are not to be used in dental practice. Instead, somewhat more pleasant substitutes are recommended in their place. Some of the tabooed words, with suggested replacements in parentheses, follow:

cost (investment)	filling (restoration)
extract (remove)	drill (prepare)
grind down (reduce)	old patient (previous patient)
cheap (inexpensive)	leaky filling (recurrent decay)
contract (payment plan)	spit (empty)
price (fee)	plates (complete dentures)

There are some places where a gentler form of language may serve a useful purpose, but when we are dealing with unpleasant truth that must be faced honestly and openly, such evasive words do not seem to serve a useful purpose.

When a person is dead he is dead, and there is no other word that says it quite as well. Many of the words used in connection with funeral service tend to build emotional detours around realities that have to be faced and accepted. We can do ourselves a service by learning to use the most direct and simple language possible in talking about the matters of death, grief and funeral service.

What can we do about unpleasant memories?

Some memories almost haunt us. They return again and again, and nothing that we do seems able to dispel them. At a time when one's ability to get through the day seems to have been sandpapered to the thinnest, a painful memory appears to threaten us with mental disaster.

But any memory is, essentially, a thought. It is the product of mental activity. And the mind can only think of one thing at a time. In short, you have control over the subject matter on which your mind focuses. At first it may not seem as if this is the case; your mind may appear to run away with you. But with practice you can prove to yourself that you can indeed take control, deciding where and on what to focus your attention. Then you can put pleasant memories in the place of unpleasant ones.

By wise planning we can help prevent the planting of unpleasant mental pictures. The picture of a person in the last throes of a wasting illness can be an immensely distressing memory; recollection of the same person in quiet repose is quite different. A useful part of the funeral procedure is the part it plays in removing some of the unpleasant memories by putting something in their place that can affirm the reality of death without overemphasizing the gruesomeness of it.

How does the funeral director help to force the reality of death on the full consciousness of a bereaved person?

The funeral director does not specifically try to force anything on the mind of a mourner. Yet the very nature of what he does professionally tends to have that effect.

First of all, the funeral director represents a function in the community that is a continual reminder of the reality of death in general. When he visits a home to take away a body, he makes this general role specific.

Second, when he sits down with the family to make the arrangements for disposition of the remains and for the funeral service, he reminds each participant that this process is definite and final. His very presence and the role he performs in the community enforce the reality of death upon the consciousness of the bereaved.

Third, when the body is properly prepared, the funeral director shows the remains as they are ready for the service and for burial or cremation. This process further enforces the idea of the reality and finality of death upon the mind and emotion of the bereaved person.

Fourth, when the time of final disposal comes and the body is committed to the earth or the fire, the funeral director by his role and his participation brings to the acts the mark of reality and finality.

Although we all harbor an inclination to deny unpleasant reality and to avoid discomfort, we ordinarily do not miss the meaning of the rites and rituals that are a part of the disposal of the dead. This fact provides a healthy basis for continuing the task of working through our grief.

FIVE

Grief's Slow Wisdom

Is any important research being done on grief
and its wise management?

The whole field of grief therapy is being actively pursued by
leading physicians, psychiatrists, clergymen and social workers.
Dr. James A. Knight, professor of psychiatry at Cornell University Medical School, writes, "Psychiatry is beginning to pay
serious attention to grief, normal and pathological, and to its
significance as one of the causative factors in the development of
psychosomatic illnesses. In fact the major direction in psychosomatic medicine today revolves around grief, loss and separation as contributing factors in the development of a multitude of
physical and emotional disorders."

A group of researchers at Harvard Medical School, under
the leadership of Dr. Eric Lindemann, includes Gerald Caplan,
whose work with emotional crises has been of major importance
in public health medicine; and Avery Weismann and Thomas
Hackett, who have written widely on death, dying, grief and
other subjects that relate to the proper management of acute
emotions.

On the West Coast, Dr. Herman Feifel, with associates in
psychiatry, psychology, sociology, anthropology and religion,
has done pioneering research, some of which was included in
the book, *The Meaning of Death,* and more of which is being
reported in papers in professional journals.

In New York a team of researchers have been studying the
bereavement of the dying person, and their findings will be

published in the spring of 1964 under the title *Counseling the Dying*. Much is being done. Much more needs to be done.

What happens when social customs change too rapidly?

Social customs are the structured form that emotions take. Because emotions are usually nonrational or superrational, these customs often serve more useful purposes for life than people usually are willing to admit. By their very nature they give invisible continuity to life, undergirding it with a stability that makes people feel comfortable with each other in their common ways of doing things, even though they may attach different and highly personal meanings to the things they do together.

When social customs change too rapidly, something important in the structure of group life is threatened. People feel that life has been pulled up by the roots, and though they may not be able to explain what it is that has happened to them, their lives show the marks of it. We see this occur when there is a rapid shifting of populations. One of the results is that people move away from old ways of doing things—ways they had accepted as normal—and are now thrown in with other people who have different and sometimes conflicting ways of doing the same things. The change in its suddenness creates uncertainty, confusion and sometimes even conflict. While Suburbia was building in America, such clashes often produced chaos.

When the social customs having to do with the ceremonial ways the community has developed for meeting death are rapidly changed or modified, the result is apt to lead to similar confusion and uncertainty. It is important to realize that social customs have a wealth of folk wisdom built into them. What may seem trivial or even irrational on the surface may be highly valid and important at the level of being, where strong emotion exists. We must show keen awareness of the underlying meanings of social custom before we dare to make changes that could cause irreparable damage.

What is a memorial society and what does it do?

A memorial society is the name given a group of people who band themselves together with the specific purpose of instituting certain reforms in funeral practice. As a group they carry on educational activities leading toward the goals they set for themselves.

Usually they charge a fee as a membership requirement, and in return for this they help their members make arrangements with funeral directors who will provide the services recommended by the society.

A prime objective of the memorial society is the setting of standard prices for the funerals of members. There may be one or more plans, so that there is one exceptionally plain ceremony, another that is more expensive, and so on. A standard, prearranged fee is the key goal—not always cost, since some memorial society plans have been more costly than regular services offered to individuals by funeral directors.

Is the memorial society program a good substitute for a traditional funeral service?

While the memorial society program satisfies the needs of a limited group of persons who have specific ideas and values, it would probably fail to meet the needs of large numbers of Americans.

Dr. Robert L. Fulton, a sociologist and professor at Los Angeles State College, has made a survey of American attitudes toward death and funeral practices. He interviewed in person and through a questionnaire a number of men and women who were members of memorial societies so that he might understand their criticisms of general funeral practice and the basis for their recommended changes. In the course of his study he found that the majority of the members of memorial societies were in upper-income brackets, were largely members of the professions, and that about a fourth of the members professed atheism, with more than half holding an atheistic view of death.

For most people, the memorial society program would not appear to be a satisfactory substitute for the traditional funeral service.

Why are some suggested reforms dangerous?

Some suggest that memorial society procedures would, if widely followed, solve any existing problems in funeral service. It is natural that laymen might arrive at such a conclusion, but it would be unwise to proceed with major reforms without knowing all that is involved. Such concern is often limited to economics, and does not consider the important needs of grief management.

From the point of view of healthful handling of grief, the procedures recommended by the memorial societies violate all five of the basic principles of grief work.

The first of these rules is to avoid the dangers of intellectualizing the emotion of grief. To "talk around" grief, to remove it from the area of emotion, is frequently but a subtle attempt to evade reality. The second rule is to keep clearly in mind that the funeral is for the bereaved and not for the deceased. Third, it is necessary to make every reasonable effort to emphasize the reality of what has happened. Fourth, it is wise to employ rites and rituals that encourage the expression of appropriate emotions. Fifth, it is urgent to bring to bear community support that can accept the emotions, confirm the reality, and give assurance for the future.

Memorial societies tend to discourage the expression of grief; they retreat into intellectualization, ignoring the important psychological benefits the funeral can give to the bereaved. They build detours around the reality of what has happened, making it difficult for the mourner to express the sorrow and fear and even the bitterness that are a part of grief. They dilute or make uncertain the support of the immediate community for the bereaved. So for these basic reasons it needs to be pointed out that this type of reform fails to meet the basic need of ceremonials for the dead, and in their stead emphasizes dangerous escapes that are already too much a part of our cultural attitude toward death.

Can our funeral customs and those of England and Denmark, say, really be compared?

It is difficult to compare the practices of a country made up of many ethnic varieties of people (who have quite different ways of doing things) with such countries as Denmark or England —both of which are small, homogeneous in population, and deeply rooted in traditions, rites and rituals commonly accepted for untold generations.

When one looks at the American scene he quickly realizes that there is no such thing as a national way of death, but that there are many ways of approaching death in America.

One could attend an Irish wake and a Jewish *Shiva* taking place within a few doors of each other in New York City. Were he to do this he would realize that he was observing ceremonial practices far apart in act and attitude, yet serving similar purposes for these people of different tradition. Such differences even show up in the fact that certain funeral homes tend to serve specific religious, cultural and ethnic groups. In this way some of the "old country" traditional ceremonies are preserved.

Life in a melting pot like the United States cannot validly be compared with cultural patterns of small European countries. It would be unfortunate if we took such comparisons so much to heart that we lost sight of the uniqueness of our country. Here we believe that there is not one right way and one wrong way of doing things, but rather that there may be many right ways.

What do you think about giving one's body for medical research?

The desire to aid in medical and scientific progress is a praiseworthy aim. Whenever we are sure that the goals we seek can be realized, the desire should be implemented.

It is important to remember that bodies vary considerably in their usefulness in scientific research. The body of a person who died of a rare disease would be of scientific importance, while that of the person who died of a common form of cancer might not be. Also it is well to note that the matter of supply and demand is at work here; while some medical schools have a constant demand for bodies for use in dissecting and anatomy classes, others are sufficiently supplied.

A most important matter to be considered concerns the sensibilities of the next of kin of the one who would so dispose of his body. Emotional responses are not always predictable. Cases are on record where relatives had acute reactions when they realized that their near kin was day after day being subject to dissection; these people were not put at ease until the remains were retrieved and interred with what they thought was proper dignity. The body of the person who dies is probably more the concern of his next of kin than of himself, and these close members of the family ought to be consulted when such action is contemplated. It should in any event be remembered that the donation of a body does not preclude a funeral service prior to donation, nor proper and reverent disposition following anatomical study.

Which is best, burial or cremation?

Actually, as far as the basic process is concerned, they are the same. One involves rapid oxidation of the body, while the other allows for a slower form of oxidation.

The matter of personal preference is determined by religious, aesthetic and practical considerations. Some religious groups advise against cremation, since they consider it to be an interference with natural processes, and so an act that may have theological implications.

Some people prefer the thought of cremation because it seems so quick, clean and efficient. Others are horrified at the rapid destruction of the physical remains of their relative or friend. Actually their own body image is involved in their feeling of horror. Some persons use cremation because they do not have a burial plot in the cemetery and because it meets their practical needs.

It probably makes no difference to the person who has died what is done with him after he is dead. The important consideration here as elsewhere are the feelings of the persons who live on and who must make their important emotional adjustments.

Is it really a help to the family to make one's own arrangements in advance?

If family circumstances are uncertain, or if there are no near relatives, it may be both useful and convenient to make one's funeral arrangements in advance. But when there are close relatives it is usually best to leave the matter of arrangements to them.

While they probably know what you would want done, that is not really the most important consideration. The key fact is that the funeral is not for the dead but for the living.

Some people say they don't care what is done with them after they are dead. Others make careful and elaborate plans for their funerals. More often the instructions left for these services say things like this, "Please keep it simple," "Don't let anyone say a lot of things about me that aren't so," or "Use one of my bright neckties." In any event, however, the process of making arrangements, of making decisions that can only be made when someone has died, are major factors in bringing the full realization of the meaning of death to one's mind and emotion. This is an important first step in wisely managing the emotional crisis that comes with death. And to deny those you love a chance to do this for you is a way of denying them the beneficial effects of acts that verify the painful reality of death.

To have an advance understanding with members of the family on matters of costs, personal preferences, and religious practices may be helpful to them when they make arrangements after your death, but you must remember that in doing their part they are in effect doing something for you which at that time will satisfy important emotional needs—among them the need to be doing as well as feeling.

SIX

The Funeral and Its Mission

Is there any easy way to handle grief?

While some ways of handling grief are much wiser than others, and far more beneficial in the long run, I know of no simple way to meet this extreme form of deprivation.

There are, however, a number of constructive things that can be done to keep the mourning process from becoming damaging.

One important thing to do is to begin to face the meaning of death in general before it comes in particular. Instead of avoiding the subject, make peace with it emotionally so that you are not caught completely off balance by inevitable events.

Another important effort to make is in understanding the nature and meaning of your own feelings when the inevitable does come. It is much easier to cope with emotions you recognize as natural and normal than it is to wonder about things and be apprehensive lest you be suffering from abnormal reactions.

If you recognize that there is a certain burden of unavoidable pain that goes along with grief, and that the sooner you face it and work it through the better off you will be, you have already taken a long step toward the wise management of the crisis. Just knowing that there are no easy escapes and emotional short cuts may be useful.

Finally, it is to be hoped that more of us will recognize that the insights of religion do much to help you fit the experiences of life into perspective. Faith enables you to see that what has happened is a part of the human predicament, not a catastrophe aimed at you in particular.

How does the church help people to prepare for death?

The church helps to make people aware of the value of life, and of the importance of living it wisely, well, and fully. When this is done, a person is continually preparing himself for the time when spirit is separated from body.

The church helps people to accept the reality of death by talking about it freely and calmly, and by recognizing the death of its members as a part of its service to the parish.

The church sings hymns that acknowledge the presence and nature of death. It reads scriptures that tell about death and yet affirm the faith that copes with death.

Perhaps more than any other institution in our culture, the church helps people to face honestly and with courage the physical limitations upon life. In so doing it helps them grasp the meaning of the spiritual quality of life that cannot be encompassed by either space or time.

Shouldn't a funeral be held in a church?

The church is a truly fitting and proper place for the final service for one of its members. The loyal member of the church has probably worshiped there through the years, was baptized there and confirmed there, was married there and took communion there. It would be the appropriate place in which to mark the end of the physical phase of his existence.

There are times, of course, when circumstance makes it difficult to conduct a service in the church. When a small number of people will be in attendance, they may feel lost and lonely in a large room; they might well feel more comfortable in the smaller room the funeral home could provide.

Moreover, we need to remember that only a minority of the people in our country are active and faithful participants in the life of any religious organization. Many among us would consider it most inappropriate to take a person's body to a church for a funeral when through his life he avoided the church.

What can be done about the grief of people who have no active religious interest or church relationship?

Millions of families in our country have no religious interest or church connection. When death comes to their families they have special problems of adjustment to make. They know that religious services usually are a part of the funeral custom, but through neglect or disbelief they have not cultivated ties that make it possible for them to arrange a religious service.

However, the emotional needs of these families are just as important as are the needs of other members of the community. When they are confronted with the ultimate mystery of life, they need understanding and comfort. It should be a matter of accepted community procedure for everyone to have the privilege of a dignified and significant ceremony at the time of death. The funeral director should feel free to call upon the clergyman he feels can best serve the needs of these bereaved people.

Sometimes coming face to face with death is a turning point in the life of a person, and the clergyman who seeks to help mourners through such distressing times may find that he stands at an open door with an opportunity for continued service to the family.

How did funeral homes get to be a part of funeral practice?

There are several factors that have contributed to the practice of using funeral homes.

Increasingly, as smaller residences were built and as apartment living became popular, it grew difficult to find the space in which to conduct a service with many people attending.

Often, when families had a funeral home available, they preferred to use it because it meant that the housekeeping chores incident to much coming and going could be turned over to the funeral director.

And as the public sought more services from the funeral director, he found that he could provide them better in a central place. Such things as an adequate parking lot became an important consideration when large numbers of persons drove to the funeral home in their own cars. Many of the services that the public now takes for granted could not be provided unless there were funeral homes for the purpose.

In many rural communities, where the church had been the traditional place for funeral services, the funeral home provided a desirable alternative, especially in the winter months, when a service in the church meant additional janitorial service and additional cost in heating the building.

In large cities the location of the funeral home became familiar to people, so that it was a convenience in making personal calls to be able to go to the more centrally located place. This was especially true when business associates and others not familiar with the home wanted to visit the family.

Thus the funeral home was developed primarily as a convenience in the community.

Does the funeral director usually own his own establishment?

In most communities in our country the funeral director owns his own establishment. In some of the larger cities there are firms that have several funeral homes.

It is interesting to note that many professional persons carry on their activities in facilities furnished by the community. The teacher has the school provided. The clergyman has a church provided. The physician carries on many of his activities in a hospital provided by the community, just as the lawyer practices his profession in a courthouse that the community maintains. The benefits of the funeral home—which the community makes use of—are usually provided by the funeral director as part of the service he makes available.

Have you ever known an unscrupulous funeral director?

I have read in newspapers of funeral directors who were called to account for what might be called malpractice, but in thirty years of parish ministry, working with many funeral directors in serving thousands of people, I have never personally known of any instance where the funeral director tried to take advantage of the grief of the bereaved for his personal advantage.

It should always be the purpose of the family to see that the funeral director serves as their agent to do what they think is right and proper and well within their means.

Are there satisfactory experiences with funeral directors that families speak about?

One proud possession of many of the funeral directors with whom I have worked is a file of letters offering gratitude for help given in a time of crisis. Usually these letters speak in general terms, since the writers themselves don't always know just what it is they want to express their thanks for.

Many of the letters that I have seen make this simple point: at a time when all was chaos and uncertainty, a calm gentleman stepped into the picture and began to bring order out of the chaos. This in itself is so important that it may signify the difference between frustration and an orderly approach to a distressing experience.

Most funeral establishments have served the public for decades; some, for several generations. Three quarters of the funeral services in the United States are repeat calls upon a funeral director who has served the family before. This gives to the funeral director-client relationship a stability and confidence that is reassuring. People know what to expect, and they know the funeral director wants to help them fulfill their needs within their resources. People would not return to the same funeral director seventy-five per cent of the time unless they wanted to. If they felt they had previously been taken advantage of, they would probably go elsewhere.

Should a clergyman help a family choose a casket?

This would depend on the clergyman, on the family, and most of all on the nature of the relationship that exists between them. If they ask his advice and counsel he should be ready and willing to give it, but from the point of view of their needs rather than of his opinions as to what their needs should be.

The pastor must of course always be available to give wise counsel to his people. His effort must always be to realize that the things they do are usually the expression of important inner feelings. His major responsibility is to understand these feelings, for only then can his counsel be truly wise.

Usually the clergyman is not called upon to offer his judgments upon the purchases a family makes. We cannot imagine his going with them to a neighborhood automobile showroom when they buy a car, to protect them in the event that a sharp automobile salesman has entered the dealer's employ. He does not go with them when they buy a new home from their realtor in order to protect them from some overzealous real estate salesman. He does not help them select a hospital room during illness, nor does he offer financial advice on matters surrounding other religious ceremonials. Nor does he usually feel inclined to pass a judgment on the funeral director in his neighborhood by trying to protect a family from possible overzealous salesmanship on the part of the funeral director.

What should be the role of the clergyman?

The clergyman, as the spiritual guide of his people, can play an especially important role in the arranging and conducting of funeral services.

His part begins well in advance of any specific service—in the education he imparts about wise and healthful procedures. It becomes specific when he is asked to counsel with the family in the midst of a crisis. He can encourage his people to call him as soon as death occurs so that he can help them meet the first full onslaught of emotion.

The clergyman should determine, with the understanding and concurrence of the family, the nature and content of the religious service.

Not only does the pastor conduct the religious service but he carries out important pastoral functions during the sometimes long and difficult period of readjustment. His task as pastoral counselor may be the most important part of his work in helping his people face and work their way through their grief.

Should a minister be paid for conducting a funeral?

A church member should be entitled to any pastoral service without thought of financial obligation. The families of the church and the funeral director should know that a fee for the services of the religious leader is not expected or desired.

When members of the community who are not regular supporters of the church ask the services of the pastor, they should make a contribution to the maintenance of the institution but it should not be construed as a payment to the pastor. No one buys the services of a pastor. They are given in the name of God, whom the pastor serves.

If members persist in making financial gifts to their pastor when they know it is neither expected nor necessary, the gift should be accepted with thanks and used as the pastor thinks would best fulfill the purposes of the giver. The gift should not be returned, for this might well be considered an offense against the emotions of the giver. His gift may be the best way he knows to say "Thank you" for services he valued and deeply appreciated.

What can religious faith do for a mourning person?

A religious faith can help to sustain the spirit of a person through the crises of life by doing three things.

First, it should help him to control his fears and anxieties by seeing life not merely in terms of its tragedy and sorrow, but also with its blessing and rich experience.

Second, it should help him to find the resources in the history and experience of man that fortify his understanding and give him a sense of the changeless in the midst of change, of the eternal in the midst of time.

Third, his faith should help him to carry his best thoughts and feelings into constructive action. Too often the best of intentions serve no purpose because the person is not able to act on them. The man of faith is inspired to act as he believes, to fulfill in his living what he aspired to in his contemplation.

When death comes near, the person of faith does not deny the facts of physical life. He does affirm the facts of the spiritual life—a life of values and meanings great enough to make a place for tragedy. The faithless life is likely to be encompassed by its tragedy, while the life of faith gathers up the tragic and transforms it by the direction of its hope and the power of its love.

While the grief of a person of faith has its pain and its disappointment, it does not lead to despair. Rather, it leads to deepened sensitivities of spirit, to higher aspirations of service and to a firmer conviction that the cosmic purpose is best understood as creative goodness.

Belief in immortality relieves some of the guilt and sorrow one would feel were he to contemplate the possibility that at no point in time or eternity could wrongs be righted or injustice rectified. Dr. Robert Laidlaw, chief of psychiatry at Roosevelt Hospital in New York City, reported recently on a study he made of persons in psychotherapy. His effort was to see whether there was any relationship between belief in immortality and progress in treatment. He found that when his patients believed in immortality, they made more rapid progress than those who did not.

What should the religious service try to do for the mourners?

A religious service should lift the focus of attention from death, tragedy and events so incident to life—not by denying them, but rather by helping to fit them into a larger perspective.

The religious service should emphasize the elements of a tradition that gives people the long view. This is usually done by reading ancient scriptures that tie present sufferings to the long-discovered sources of spiritual strength.

The religious service should emphasize the importance of a living faith that can give courage in the present and direction for the future.

The religious service should provide evidence of group strength available to the individual who is weakened by sorrow and in need of the strength of others during his period of trial.

The religious service should recognize the dignity of life and the validity of the feelings that people feel in the face of death.

SEVEN

Ceremonials, Death and Dignity

Why do some people joke about funerals, funeral directors and graveyards?

The grim events that have to do with death are charged with both mystery and anxiety, and some of us sometimes gain emotional release by being able to make light of them. So we have cartoons to make the political crises seem less foreboding. We have comedies to make light of the problems of life that distress people. We tell jokes to shake loose the accumulated tensions that gather inside us, and nothing gives a sense of release like a good belly laugh.

Through humor we feel that we gain some mastery over the things that may really master us. We know that we cannot ultimately master or deny death, but at least we make it less of an emotional hazard by taking some part of the subject and holding it up for ridicule, sarcasm or biting humor. Because the funeral director is the symbol of death in the community he is an ever-present target for this kind of humor.

Perhaps he does not realize it, but one of his most useful functions is to give a focal point for the anxieties that can be released through the humor of which he is the target. But we actually do not laugh at the funeral director. We laugh at and with ourselves and use him as a convenient way of doing it.

Why would anyone want to become a funeral director?

Many funeral directors are following in a family tradition, and have inherited both their interest and their establishments.

Some became funeral directors quite by accident, as did the college student who took a part-time job in a funeral home and then became so interested in the work that he never left it. Increasingly, people are attracted to the profession by a desire to do service work that is needed and valued by the community.

Does the funeral director have an easy job?

I suppose we are all inclined to think that the other person has the easy job. This is usually because we do not see all that is involved in what he does.

The community assigns to the funeral director one of the most difficult of tasks, that of ministering to people who are faced with the fact of death—a fact for which they have generally had little cultural preparation. Funeral directors are obliged to deal with the most morbid and gruesome aspects of community life—the suicides, the accidents, and the end results of long and devastating illness. There are few things about their work in which they can show pride. While a fur salesman can brag about the sale of an expensive mink coat, the funeral director cannot take a similar attitude toward a funeral. Like the doctor or the lawyer, he cannot reveal confidences about his professional activities. When his friends are ill he does not feel right about going to call on them because he knows what he represents as well as they do. And if he advertises in a local paper he must do it with discretion because his services, though ultimately essential, are something people want to avoid for themselves and those they love.

While there are compensations in being able to serve people in times of personal crises, it would take quite an agile imagination to make one think that the funeral director has an easy job.

Are funeral directors highly regarded in other countries?

People almost always and everywhere have had mixed feelings about funeral directors. They don't want to have to call a

funeral director because this is done only on the death of someone dear or near. Yet when death does occur, they want the
funeral director immediately. This is a conflicting attitude, but
it is not something new.

In ancient Egypt the art of embalming was highly prized for
religious reasons, but the embalmer was looked down upon.
When someone died the embalmer was summoned, and when
he had finished his work he was paid a fancy fee. Then the
friends and relatives gathered about the door to stone the
hapless creature as he tried to make his escape in a shower of
missiles. There has always been something of this attitude visi-
ble in our relationship to funeral directors. We value the service
they perform, but we resent the circumstances that make it
necessary. Often we take out our resentment against them by
modern equivalents of throwing stones; in more refined communities it may be nothing more than a sly joke or a subtle dis-
crimination in social matters.

The practices in various countries differ according to custom
and tradition. Usually, however, the person who cares for the
bodies of the dead is granted a type of grudging respect. In
some countries he is given a place of special honor, while in
others he has a menial role in the life of the community.

In our country the funeral director is usually judged by the
reputation he has built for himself. He is known by most people
in his community, and usually has been engaged in his profession for a long time. If he provides the services people desire
they approve of him, and if he does not he is sure to suffer the
consequences.

Is funeral service a profession or a business?

In some parts of the country the degree of professional training
is greater than in others. Some states require certain college
courses as a prerequisite for licensing. In other states the requirements may be considerably less. Just as the requirements for

teachers or clergymen vary in different parts of the country, so they do with funeral directors.

While the amount of training required has important bearing on the professional status of the individual funeral director, the basic approach of the funeral director to the public also goes a long way toward setting the nature of his status in the community. If a funeral director is primarily concerned with providing the merchandise for funeral services, he would be considered primarily a businessman, with his professional acts as secondary and incidental. If, however, his primary concern is in providing an important and skilled service to the community, with the merchandise a secondary consideration, then the professional status would be paramount.

The history of every professional group has been a record of lifting standards from within the profession at the same time that the community was seeking more adequate services for its own needs. A hundred years ago a physician learned the practice of medicine by accompanying an older doctor on his daily rounds. Much progress has been made in a hundred years in medicine. The truly professional funeral director is concerned with raising the educational and professional standards of his profession. However, there are still some who are quite satisfied to think of what they do as primarily a business relationship.

Do you think funeral directors should advertise in the local newspapers?

It is generally considered unprofessional to place advertisements in the public press calling attention to professional services. So it is that doctors, dentists, and lawyers do not use this type of advertising. Businessmen, however, think it perfectly proper to use advertising to sell their products. The use of public advertising is one of the practices that tends to mark funeral service more as a business than as a profession.

**How do you feel about putting so much money
in the ground?**

Actually, at a funeral no money is put into the ground. People
pay money for things they use in the process of interring a body.
If we keep in mind that it is the body that is put into the ground,
we more easily keep our thinking straight.

Some of us seem determined to decide how other people
should spend their money; this is quite a common pastime. Some
people think it is a crime that others burn up ten billion dollars'
worth of money a year in cigarette smoking. Still other people
consider it shameful that Americans spend twenty billion dollars a year to take a special kind of sedative called alcohol.
Others feel it is unfortunate that billions of dollars are spent
on gambling. But these are personal judgments and matters of
opinion. As long as people are people, they will go on spending
money as they see fit.

The satisfaction a person gains through providing what he
feels is a fitting funeral service is a matter of personal choice,
and though I might disagree with him, it is not my right or privilege to determine how he should spend his money.

Then too, conditions change as we ourselves become involved.
What I might consider a waste of money when I look at it casually and free from emotional involvement may look quite
different when it is a service I am arranging for someone I
loved. To judge the value of a service by the matter of costs
alone seems rather inadequate.

Should a person go into debt for a funeral?

Some people never buy anything unless they can pay for it in
cash. Others are continually using in the present what they will
pay for in the future, and each year many billions of dollars'
worth of contracts are written by men and women who buy
cars, homes, appliances, vacations and even their marriages on

the installment plan. Wisely handled debt is encouraged rather than discouraged by American business methods.

When persons are called on to arrange a funeral, they are sometimes obliged to ask the funeral director to help them meet an immediate crisis with the understanding that payment will be made in the future. We seldom realize how much money is advanced by funeral directors. In effect they run a private banking service for people who are faced with the problems of death and the disposal of physical remains.

It would be emotionally distressing for a person who never incurred debts to have to go into debt for a funeral or anything else. On the other hand, in our society the practice of delayed payment is so common that it presents no emotional obstacles to those involved. The important matter to be considered here is not so much the matter of the incurring of the debt itself as what can be done to help persons effectively meet the crises of their lives. If debt is an aid in doing that, the debt may be good. If it becomes a deeply depressing burden, then it is not good.

What does a breakdown of funeral costs show?

Any breakdown of funeral costs shows first that there is a great deal of variation both in regard to regional factors and to personal preferences. People can select a funeral with all the necessary equipment and usual services even if they are aided by the welfare program of the community in matters of general support. One can also spend large amounts on funerals, but people usually do not do so. The average cost for an adult funeral in the United States is in the neighborhood of $2,300, plus vault, if used, and cemetery charges.

It is interesting to note that there are usually more socially-provided sources of financial assistance in meeting funeral costs than for any other major expense one incurs in life. Social security, veteran's benefits, union and lodge benefits, and industrial and personal insurance programs frequently pay all or a major part of the costs of funeral services.

It is misleading to include the costs of the flowers that are sent by relatives, friends and business associates as part of the funeral cost. While they do cost money, the money is spent by others than those who are obliged to meet the costs of the funeral itself. The flowers are most often the warmest way people know to express their sympathy, and for many symbolize the flowering of new life even where there is death.

Do funerals reflect American ways of thinking and acting?

One has only to look closely at funeral practice in America to see how much of it is a reflection of our attitudes and practices generally. The commendable and important contributions Americans make to funeral practice are also reflections of admirable qualities in our patterns of living. The objectionable things about funeral activity are projections of objectionable ways of thinking and acting in other phases of cultural life.

The wide differences in funeral customs are indications of the ways in which group life in different parts of the country influence funeral customs. The stolid New Englander goes quietly home after a funeral, while the rural Midwesterner returns to the church for a feast spread by neighbors. The family with Italian or other Mediterranean roots will engage in strong expressions of emotion, while those of Scottish or Swedish descent will carefully guard their feelings and do all they can to hold them in check.

For persons who are "status conscious," the funeral will quite naturally bear the marks of their interest in status symbols. Those who find security in simplicity and quiet dignity will use the type of service that makes them feel secure. The American interest in progress and general improvement of methods and equipment shows up in the materials that surround funeral practice. It makes little difference whether a grave is dug by a man who spends all day at the task or by a mechanical device that does the same work in half an hour. A grave is a grave, and it fulfills the same function. Whether a funeral home is a simple place in a rural village or a pretentious building in a large city, it serves its main purpose when it furnishes the services which make it possible for a family to face death and to prepare to face a changed life.

Funerals, like graduations, weddings and other ceremonials, tend to reflect both the good and the bad, the wise and the foolish in the cultural surroundings.

What makes a practice "pagan"?

We occasionally hear the charge that funerals tend to be expressions of paganism. The term "pagan" as used here implies that the values which are the basis for judgment are materialistic rather than spiritual, and that the philosophy of life that is reflected is degrading rather than uplifting as far as the idea of the nature of man is concerned.

I believe that to determine whether a funeral is good or bad merely on the basis of dollar and cents criteria is pagan. It measures a social, religious and personal process on the basis of cost accounting. This is an inadequate standard of judgment. The rites and rituals men employ at times of personal crisis invariably have about them a superrational quality that cannot be measured by materialistic standards.

No one really has the right to label the motivations of another by the materialistic judgments he chooses, for such approaches usually fail to take into consideration the meanings that the participants attach to the processes. It is like saying that it is a waste of money for a bride to spend all that money on a beautiful white dress that she will never wear again, especially when she has a whole closet full of lovely clothes from which to choose. The statement is factually true, but it fails to

take into account the proud joy of the bride and the importance
of the ceremonial for her.

The term "pagan" is one of those weighted words that is
more often misused than not. It must be used with care, since
it can mislead the reader as well as the user.

Should there be changes and reform in funeral practices?

The process of change has been going on continuously. Much
of the change has been for the better; some has been for the
worse. The word "reform" implies a value judgment, however.
And that is dangerous; a number of the things one person
thinks are "reforms" for the better may very well be considered
by another to be changes for the worse.

One of the changes for the worse that I have observed in all
of American life—and in funeral service also—is a trend toward secularization, where things are determined by material
standards rather than by spiritual judgment. Even those who
criticize funeral practice as "pagan" usually make their judgments from a secular, materialistic point of view.

One of the changes for the better is the growing awareness
of the fact that funerals are increasingly for the living and not
for the dead. This gives a new sensitivity to what is happening
to the emotions of people. More careful studies in psychiatry,
sociology and pastoral care will help to give direction to this
concern for people.

Any social institution is in constant movement, and therefore needs examination for what it does, and how and why.
That is why the Roman Catholic Church called its ecumenical
council meetings—to examine the institution and to modify it
as necessary to meet new conditions.

As a body of social practice, funeral custom also should be
carefully and continually examined, and modified as necessary
to meet the changing panorama of American life.

Some of the changes likely to come would have to do with

professional training of funeral directors, to help them bring to their work a more adequate understanding of the psychological factors involved in the working through of grief.

Some of the change would have to do with specific practices, such as the closed casket during all religious services whether in church or in the funeral home.

Some would have to do with the use of language that says what it means instead of contributing to ambiguity and evasion.

Some of the most needed changes would have to do with the general American attitude toward death and dying, ideas that grow out of our glorification of youth, beauty and health.

Until we make a place in our national outlook for maturity, aging, and the withering-away phase of the cycle of life, we will not be able to undergird life with an adequate philosophy of life and death.

What new trends do you hope to see in funeral practice in the years ahead?

I hope to see a growing freedom of exchange of ideas among the professions doing research in the psychosomatic and social meaning of grief. I hope to find a growing interest on the part of the general public in the meaning of funeral ceremonies and their place in the wise handling of their grief. I hope to see a growing skill in all the caretaking professions, in helping to understand and manage the emotional crises of life.

Similarly I hope to see research grants made available for detailed and significant studies of grief, funeral practices and the related field of human emotion.

Recently I completed a study conducted with a psychiatrist, a psychoanalyst, and a clinical psychologist of an important phase of death and dying. Such professional collaborations give breadth and depth to research, and in the field of grief the multiprofessional type of work seems to be particularly fruitful. I would hope that many other research teams would go to work on specific aspects of the subject so that we can grow in our understanding of this vast and important aspect of human behavior.

What do psychiatrists think about the funeral service?

A psychiatrist, James A. Knight, M.D., writes, "Physicians, clergymen, and funeral directors should understand thoroughly the steps in the normal grief reaction—in which the work of mourning must be done, the bondage to the deceased broken, and new relationships formed. The rituals and customs associated with death and dying should be understood and evaluated from the standpoint of how well they help people do the necessary work of mourning and how well they succeed in preventing pathological grief reactions which now or later lead to illness."

A psychiatrist, Eric Lindemann, M.D., writes, "The funeral service is psychologically necessary in order to give the opportunity for 'grief work.' The bereaved must be given the capacity to work through his grief if he is to come out of that situation emotionally sound. Finally we need to see to it that those whom we serve are left with comforting memories. Some will argue this point. I think, however, it is sound psychologically." Then he adds these words, "It is in this region that an alliance with the profession of funeral directors is just as important, if not more important, for psychiatrists, than working with their colleagues in other medical disciplines."

What do religious leaders think of the value of funerals and the services of funeral directors?

Most clergymen conduct hundreds of funerals, and so have a chance to evaluate the attitudes and practices of funeral directors. They know that some are more competent than others, but they know this to be true about their own colleagues as well. Perhaps they can best speak for themselves.

A Jewish clergyman, Dr. Nathan Perilman, says, "Many people who approach a funeral with dread lest they be part of a barbarous rite, find themselves grateful to the man who creates the background of a ceremony that has grace and dignity and beauty. Where that background is properly set, the family is best served and the efforts of the minister who brings the consolation of faith will bear the most fruitful results."

A Roman Catholic priest, the Rev. Daniel A. Lord, S.J., said, "I bow respectfully to undertakers, morticians, funeral directors or whatever they call themselves these days. They are a gentle and considerate profession. They are men who have been trained to take the grimness from the business of death. There is something a little priestly about their ministrations. You feel that they have that reverence for the body which presupposes a faith in its resurrection."

A Protestant minister, the Rev. Jack D. Forest, writes, "This then is what the funeral is for: the worship of God and aid to the mourner. There can be no more certain guide as to what is 'right' or 'wrong' in a funeral than one's understanding of the people who are confronted with death."

EIGHT

Some Concluding Thoughts

The ordered ways of doing things give us security. The fact that certain actions are expected of us draws us into activity that our damaged spirits could not otherwise easily initiate. So it is that custom and ritualized acts have their own deep wisdom. They give meaning and movement to life when those qualities are most needed.

Any examination of funeral custom and practice must start at the point of deep personal and group needs. It is futile to theorize about such practices in the abstract, for each funeral is unique in its relation to one's personal and group history.

A startling hazard of theorizing about funerals is that we tend to intellectualize what cannot be. Feelings have their own validity, and that validity must be recognized. When the fabric of life is disrupted by cruel circumstance, the energy of men must be directed toward repairing the rents so that life may move forward again.

So it becomes quite obvious that our actions at such times are based on our emotional and community needs. The funeral rites are really for the bereaved, and not for the deceased. We grieve because of what has happened to us. We express our feelings because we have them and cannot do otherwise. We develop ceremonies to surround the event because we must make sure that our deepest needs are recognized and met.

It is at this point that the full strength of our religious faith asserts itself. We are creatures of faith, and could not live a day without expressing it. But special events in life demand special expressions of our faith. Faith in the value of a life that is not measured by space and time is a religious act. Through it we gain assurance concerning the meaning of our own life, and thus find strength to carry on even when the days distress us. Religion is the reality-affirming, personality-verifying process in life.

Our deep feelings are not easily expressed alone. Our grief is a social act, for it verifies the values we place upon life within the fabric and structure of the community. We burst into tears more easily when we see others crying. We are aware of some feelings only as we experience them within the life of a group. Funerals are group events wherein the reality and validity of our sorrow, pain and distress are recognized as shared experiences. The funeral brings together a group of persons who have common feelings, who support each other in the act of pouring out their emotions.

Through such rites we move beyond the things we know to face the great mysteries that surround life. Just as it is difficult to know when life begins—at birth, at the point where the foetus is recognized as human, at conception or at some point where biological endowment asserts itself—so also it is difficult to be sure about the time and nature of death. Is it an exact moment, or is it a process of transition? No one really knows, but we do know that the being who was alive continues to bear a resemblance in death. We pay our tribute to life itself through the respect we show for the physical remains that continue to show the marks of the identity we have known and cherished even as we relinquish it. Therefore the deeper meanings of the rites, rituals and ceremonials that surround death must be known and understood in order that we may find in them the values they reveal for the living.

In his introduction, Dr. Knight wrote from the point of view of a physician, a psychiatrist and a teacher of psychiatrists. His concern for the wise and effective handling of the life crises that come with grief and bereavement grows out of his interest in psychosomatic medicine and research.

While I concur with Dr. Knight's insight into grief—and value his judgment highly, and appreciate his wisdom—my experience personally and professionally has grown from a different relationship to people. As a pastor, I have been called upon to interpret the emotional, religious and spiritual meanings of death. I have walked with many people through "the valley of the shadow of death." I have tried to make it possible for these men, women and youngsters to find the meaning of the words of Jesus, who said, "Blessed are they that mourn for they shall be comforted." Comfort grows from strength, not weakness. The processes that contribute to that comfort are valued for the strength that they give. This is why we value the community and religious ceremonials that recognize and serve the deepest emotional needs of its members. It is a form of spiritual insurance, made available when most needed.

Let us each in our own way look carefully at the religious and community actions with which we surround our times of crisis, for these are the ways by which we work through our essential needs. These acts, with their innate wisdom, sustain the soul and channel our pain, anguish and distress into healthful forms of expression. Then life can restore itself, regroup its energies, and face its tomorrows with faith, hope and courage.

About the Author:

EDGAR N. JACKSON has had nine years of experience in clinical work in addition to his thirty years as a parish minister. His undergraduate study at Ohio Wesleyan University was followed by eight years of graduate work at Drew Seminary, Union Theological Seminary, Yale Divinity School, and the Postgraduate Center for Psychotherapy in New York.

Dr. Jackson is the author of many books, and has contributed articles to religious, professional and secular journals. His last six books were selected for distribution by book clubs serving the American ministry.

He lectures widely at colleges, universities, seminaries, and pastors' conferences, as well as at the Army Chaplain's School and before the American Foundation of Religion and Psychiatry. A far wider audience hears him through his many radio and television appearances. Dr. Jackson has probably written and lectured more than has any other person on the subjects considered in this little book.